DENIM UPCYCLED

DENIM UPCYCLED

BREATHE NEW LIFE INTO OLD JEANS

JANET GODDARD

First published 2023 by
Guild of Master Craftsman Publications Ltd
Castle Place, 166 High Street, Lewes,
East Sussex, BN7 1XU

ISBN 978-1-78494-644-9

A catalogue record for this book is available from
the British Library.

Managing Art Editor: Darren Brant
Art Editor: Jennifer Stephens
Editor: Wendy Hobson
Photography: Sian Irvine
Stylist: Sian Irvine

Colour origination by GMC Reprographics
Printed and bound in China

contents

introduction

Denim jeans are ubiquitous and iconic. Starting life as hard-wearing work clothes, they have changed and developed to the point where you would be hard-pressed to walk down any high street without seeing a good few people wearing denim jeans. And not just jeans – jackets, dresses, bags and hats are all made from this wonderful fabric.

What is denim and what makes it so special?

Denim is not the item of clothing but the fabric from which it is made. It is a cotton fabric but whereas other cotton has a straight warp and weft – the threads running down the length and across the width of the fabric respectively – denim differs in several ways.

- It is made using heavier yarn.

- The weft threads in denim are white while the warp threads are traditionally indigo, although many more colours are now available.

- Denim is woven in a twill weave in which the warp threads go diagonally under two threads and over one, hence the differences in colour on either side of the fabric.

The result is a natural cotton fabric that is sturdy but comfortable, hard-wearing and water-resistant, keeps its shape and is less likely to wrinkle, is stain and odour resistant so needs less washing but is washable at high temperatures if necessary. As a natural material, it is also suitable for vegans (no animals are harmed or killed during the creation or manufacturing of denim). No wonder we love it so much!

Modern denim clothes

While traditional denim is a natural fabric, your favourite jeans might well contain other products, including some synthetic fibres such as Lycra and Spandex, giving the fabric additional stretch. Your jeans might also be in many more colours than the traditional indigo.

Why the book?

Denim, and jeans in particular, have become such a wardrobe staple that most people end up with at least one or two pairs of denim jeans that don't fit any more, have worn out in places or have gone out of style. Denim is a durable and versatile fabric, so in this book I will show you how to repurpose and upcycle pre-loved denim into stylish and useful items for you, your family and friends, or your home. Maybe you could also encourage those who are not creative with a needle to hand over their old jeans to you – or at least to a charity shop!

There are so many benefits to making use of available resources in this way.

We have all known for some time that we need to make the way we behave more sustainable to avoid the predicted climate changes. While addressing our wardrobes in a different way is a mere drop in the ocean, it does represent a mindset that we can apply across other areas too. Every contribution is a positive step.

Throw-away society has to be made a thing of the past. Our new watchwords are sustainable, repurpose, recycle, upcycle. This book is all about releasing those possibilities from a simple pair of jeans!

Upcycling, downcycling and repurposing our waste are key if we are to minimize what we put into landfill and preserve energy and resources. Instead of just getting rid of items we no longer have a use for, we need to remind ourselves of the energy, resources and raw materials that have gone into each product and let that prompt our ingenuity to find ways to give it a new purpose, thus saving resources and helping to build a greener future.

There are benefits to be had on a personal level, too. We can create some fun and beautiful items for ourselves and our friends and family. Nothing shows you care more than a unique handmade gift. We can enjoy applying our creative skills, learning new techniques and keeping alive the skills of our grandparents. We can lose ourselves in the moment, helping us to relax from everyday stresses (without spending a fortune in the process). Then there is the fun to be had being on the lookout for source materials in sales, the remnant bin in your sewing shop or items in local charity shops and thrift stores, where we can save money while supporting local businesses and local and national charities. Being imaginative is wonderful and letting your denim finds inspire your creativity ensures that your designs are unique and personal.

There's really no need for landfill to be overwhelmed with unwanted jeans when they still have so many more incarnations to go through.

A brief history of blue jeans

When you think of denim, you think of jeans – they go hand in hand. The term 'denim' derives from the French 'serge de Nîmes', serge being a sturdy fabric from that French town where it is widely believed denim originated. With the combination of excellent properties, the French weavers realized they had developed a unique fabric. Yet the fabric is no longer produced anywhere in France.

It was in the USA that the newly baptized fabric, denim, really came to life.

In 1853 a German immigrant moved from New York to California to set up a Western branch of his family's dry goods business which, among many other products, imported denim fabric. His name was to become synonymous with jeans throughout the world: Levi Strauss.

One of his customers was a tailor called Jacob W. Davis, who began making hard-wearing denim workwear for the gold miners. Introducing rivets, patented in 1873, improved their durability still further and the two men entered a partnership.

They began making overalls in the 1870s and the company created its first pair of jeans in the 1890s. It was not until 1905 that any competition appeared, with Wrangler in 1905 and Lee in 1911.

Denim jeans continued to grow in popularity, mainly as workwear, until the 1940s. Durable, comfortable and associated with working culture, in the 1950s jeans began to increase in popularity among younger people with the advent of teenage culture until they eventually reached their current iconic status.

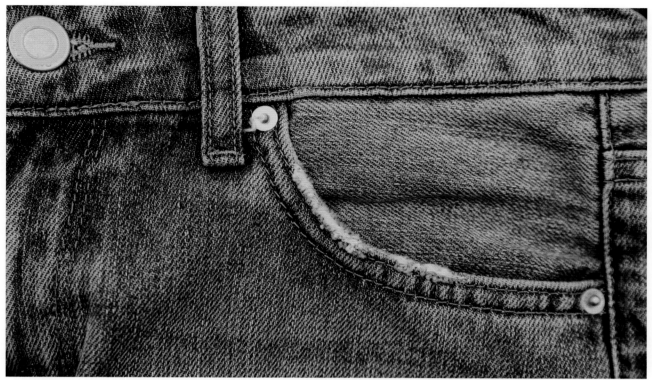

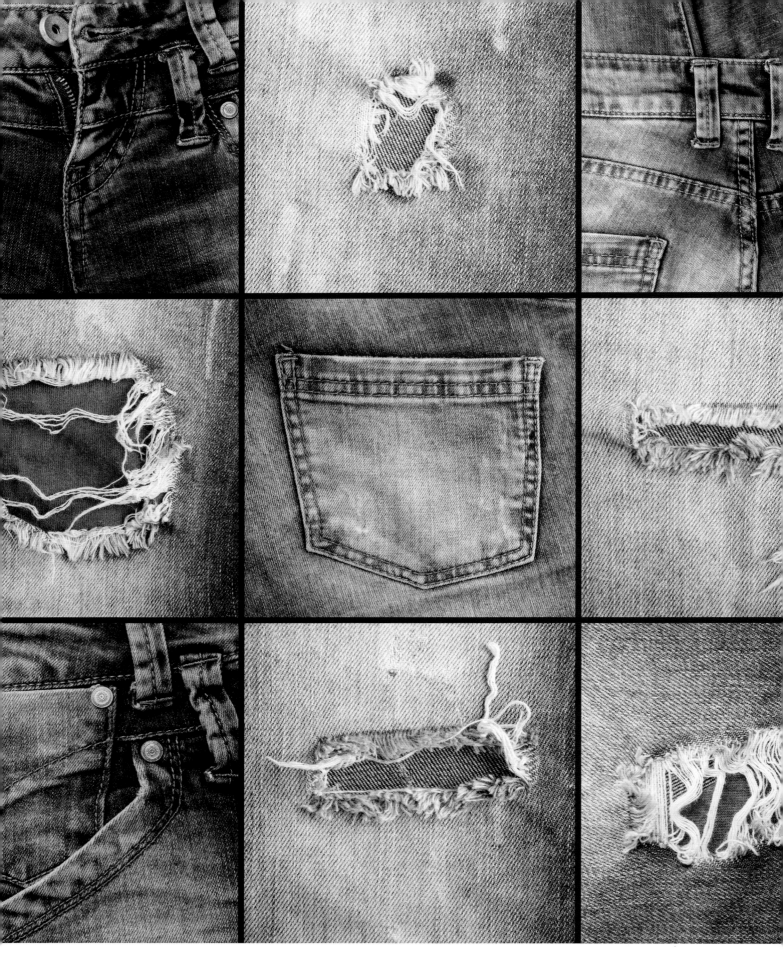

deconstructing your jeans

You can use any denim garments for the projects in this book, from your own outgrown or outworn items to things picked up in a charity shop or given to you.

Washing and cleaning

If you are reusing your own denim items you will know they have been washed and whether there are any worn or stained areas but if you have been given a piece of clothing or purchased it from a charity shop, then the first thing to do is wash the item. Check them for dirty marks, ripped areas, holes and worn areas. Cut away and discard any dirty or soiled areas, but don't get rid of ripped pieces, holes or worn areas as you may be able to incorporate them in your designs.

Selecting and cutting

Before you cut into the garment, think about what you are going to make, otherwise you may find that the parts that you have cut, you really need in one piece!

I found that for the majority of projects I cut up the centre leg seam with a very sharp pair of scissors, around the crotch and down the other side to open out the leg sections and to get the largest pieces of denim. I then cut pieces from the jeans as I needed them. The pocket sections are really useful and when cutting these it is important to allow at least 1in (2.5cm) of flat denim all the way around the pocket for seam allowances. Sometimes a project will need a leg section of a pair of jeans and in this case you would need to cut the leg away from the top of the jeans in one piece.

Because denim is a thick fabric, I generally cut on either side of a seam rather than try to sew through too many layers, but occasionally you may want to unpick a seam, in which case a seam ripper is the best tool to use.

Belt loops are very thick and sometimes too thick to stitch over on a domestic sewing machine, especially if you are wanting to add another layer of denim to the top of them. If this is the case I often unpick the top of the belt loop, unfold it, lay it flat and stitch it into the seam. Sometimes it is not possible to do this and it is best just to discard the loop altogether.

If the seam has an overlocking thread, turn the top side facing you – that will have two lines of parallel stitches running through looped stitches. Cut though every few stitches, then gently pull the loop threads to undo the seam.

Save everything

Save every piece of denim. As I cut up items and accumulate scraps of denim, I toss them all into a storage basket. When I then come to make a new project, I always start by looking at my pile of scraps to see what I can use from my basket, and sometimes adapt the items to suit. In projects in this book I have used both front and back pockets in the bags and storage items, cut-away thick seams have been used for hanging loops, a folded hem for a necklace, a waistband for a bracelet, and tiny pieces stitched together for a drawstring bag. Even after making all the projects for this book I will still have a basket of denim scraps which I will continue to use in further projects.

other materials

There are a number of other fabrics and materials you will need for your projects.

Fabrics

One of the nicest parts of starting a new project is being able to choose the fabrics. I have made fabric choices to suit the project. If the project uses large shapes I have tended to use fabric that has a larger-scale print design; for smaller shapes the fabric print has tended to be smaller as well. All the projects in this book use fabric that is 100 per cent cotton and of a high quality.

The fabrics used in this book are bright, modern and there are a variety of patterns. Each project details the fabric colour and print I have used but you can substitute your own fabric choices to suit your taste.

Measurements have been given for each piece of extra fabric used so you may find that you have some suitable fabrics to hand in your scrap bag. The measurements detailed are precise so there will not be any fabric left over.

Fusibles

Fusible web is a heat-activated adhesive that allows you to use an iron to bond fabrics together. I have used a light-weight fusible web in some projects, mostly those that have an appliquéd element. Most varieties of fusible web are paper backed, which allows you to draw or trace your motifs onto the adhesive and then bond to the fabric.

Fusible interfacing adds a firmness to items and I have used single-sided fusible interfacing in a couple of projects. It works in the same way as fusible web in that it is heat activated and is ironed to the wrong side of the fabric during construction.

Fusible wadding is a great product as it adds texture to your project. I have used fusible wadding in the tablet storage pouch and also the zippy pouch to provide a protective element – plus it looks great when quilted.

Thread and other notions

A selection of navy, blue, black, and dark and light grey threads are the most useful colours for piecing. I tend to use a high-quality 50 weight thread for general piecing. In addition, embroidery threads have been used to embellish and decorate projects and a variety of colours have been used to complement and contrast with the denim. You can use whatever colours suit your scheme.

Everything you need in the way of fastenings – such as zips, magnetic snap fasteners and so on – is listed at the top of each project.

equipment

Good-quality basic equipment is needed to make these projects. There is no need to spend a fortune on the latest gadgets, just invest in some good-quality essential resources.

Sewing machine: The most important piece of equipment is a sewing machine as almost all the projects are worked by machine. It really only needs to be able to stitch forwards and backwards and doesn't need a whole lot of fancy stitches, although a zigzag stitch can be handy for neatening seams. This usually comes as standard on modern machines.

It is important that your machine is cared for and is cleaned and serviced regularly to keep it working well. A little oil applied according to the manufacturer's instructions should help to keep everything in good order. Changing the needle regularly also helps with the quality of stitching, so I usually change the machine needle every time I begin a new project. The machine feet used the most are the standard straight stitch foot and the zipper foot for stitching in zips.

Rulers: These come in many shapes and sizes, are marked in inches or centimetres and are made of tough acrylic. I personally find the rulers with yellow markings the easiest to see on fabric but this is a personal choice.

Scissors: A sharp pair of dressmaking scissors is essential for cutting fabric. A medium-size pair is useful for cutting off corners and trimming, while a small pair is handy for snipping threads.

Pins: I use flat flower head fine pins or glass-headed pins as they help to keep the fabric flat, but any type of pin will be fine.

Needles: For denim, I generally use a jeans 130/705 sewing machine needle. Hand-sewing needles are used for some finishing off techniques and are available in many sizes. Sharps are good for general sewing and hand stitching binding.

Clips: These are great for holding multiple layers together when hand stitching or top stitching around the top of a bag. The clips are plastic (think mini clothes pegs but better) and can be removed easily as you stitch.

Fabric markers: There are many fabric markers available but any marker should be easy to use, easy to see and simple to remove after you have finished sewing. Markers are used to mark measurements for cutting or stitching and also quilting lines or patterns. Several different coloured markers are needed in order to contrast with both light and dark fabrics. White and silver markers, water-erasable pens and chalk markers are all useful.

Fabric glue pen: Sometimes it is really helpful to add a dab of fabric glue before stitching two pieces of fabric together, especially if they are small or in a tricky place and you need them a little more secure than just held with a pin.

Seam ripper: This is often called a 'quick unpick' and usually comes as a tool with the sewing machine. Hugely useful for removing tacking (basting) stitches or the odd mistake we all make now and then, it can also be used to unpick seams.

Iron and ironing board: After the sewing machine, the iron is the most useful tool. A good-quality iron and a firm, clean ironing board are needed for all the projects.

It is worth pressing seams with a dry iron as you go, especially if you have pieced together more than one denim shape. Then give the item a good press when you have finished. It will make all the difference to the finished product.

stitching denim

Most of the projects are completed with simple machine stitching but some require a little hand stitching or embroidery. These have been kept to the minimum but give the projects a nice finish.

Basic piecing

Basic piecing involves stitching two shapes together using a standard straight stitch on the machine and the standard presser foot. The raw edges of the shapes must be aligned precisely for an accurate finish. A backstitch at the beginning and end of a seam will secure the thread. All seams are ¼in (6mm) wide.

Finishing seams

For added strength, some seams have been finished with a zigzag stitch or another row of straight stitching. If this has been necessary, it has been added to the pattern instructions so you will see it as you read them through.

Machine top stitching

Many of the projects use top stitching as a decorative feature or to hold fast a finished edge, such as the top of a bag or a pocket. Either way, neat and even top stitching helps to improve the appearance of a project and often helps it to lay flat. Each pattern explains what distance the stitched line should be away from the finished edge and usually it is either ⅛in (3mm) or ¼in (6mm). You can use your standard presser foot on your sewing machine or alternatively a zipper foot or edge stitch foot. The key to neat top stitching is keeping the distance from the finished edge as even as possible.

Measurements and templates

I have used imperial as the standard measurement throughout all my patterns, but the metric measurements have been included as well. Use either imperial or metric, and do not mix the two together.

All the cutting instructions for the projects include a ¼in (6mm) seam allowance.

All the templates for projects can be found at the back of the book (pages 130–133) and are printed at full size. They have all been reversed for transferring to the wrong side of the fabrics.

Machine appliqué

In this book, I have used simple raw edge machine appliqué, although you could stitch by hand if you prefer. The raw edges of the shapes will fray slightly, creating a soft effect.

1 Trace the motif onto the paper side of the fusible web. If the motif has several parts, each part must be traced separately.

2 Roughly cut around each traced motif.

3 Place the fusible web motifs onto the reverse of your chosen fabrics so that the paper side is facing you and iron the motif to the fabric.

4 Cut out each motif neatly along the traced lines.

5 Peel the backing paper away from the motif and position it onto your project fabric. Overlap the part motifs where necessary. Iron in place.

6 Using a straight stitch on the sewing machine and a matching or contrasting thread, top stitch close to the outer edge of the motifs.

hand sewing and embroidery stitches

Hand sewing is used in these projects mainly for finishing and embellishment.

Starting a stitch

To begin an embroidery stitch use an 'away knot' on the front of the work. An away knot is worked 3–5in (7.6–12.7cm) away from the area where the embroidery begins. Tie a knot at the end of the thread you are working with and take the needle down through the front of the fabric to the back, about 3–5in (7.6–12.7cm) away from where your first stitch is to begin. A long thread will be secured on the back of the work. After the stitch is completed, cut off the knot from the front of the work and thread the long thread onto the needle and weave it securely under the stitches on the back of the embroidery.

Ending a stitch

Take the thread to the wrong side of your work and weave it under the worked stitches for about 2in (5cm). Try to keep the wrong side of your work as neat as possible.

Slip stitch

A slip stitch is used to secure a finished edge, such as a hand appliquéd shape or binding, invisibly to another fabric. Catch a thread from under the fabric with a needle; at the same time catch a single thread on the fold of the fabric. Repeat, keeping the stitches as even as possible.

Running stitch

If you know how to hand sew at all, you know how to do a running stitch! Working from right to left, bring the needle up at A, go in at B and come back out at C. Continue in this manner, spacing stitches evenly. To end the stitch, go down through the fabric to the wrong side at B.

Backstitch

This is a strong stitch that can be used either for hand stitching seams or as a decorative stitch to create a solid line, anywhere you need to 'draw' with a thread. Working from right to left, bring the needle up at A and make a small backwards stitch by going down at B. Bring the needle through at C. Move the needle to the left under the fabric. Continue this pattern, bringing the needle up a space ahead and down into the hole made by the last stitch. To end the stitch, go down through the fabric to the wrong side at A. Stitches should be about ⅛in (3mm). They will appear continuous on the right side but overlapped on the wrong side of the fabric.

Cross stitch

Two stitches that cross each other to form an X, cross stitch can be worked individually or in rows.

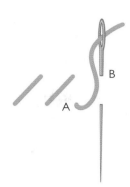

1 Working from left to right, bring the needle up at A and down at B. If you are working a row of cross stitches, continue working slanted stitches evenly in this manner.

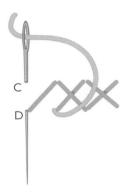

2 On the return, work from right to left, crossing over the first stitches from C to D, forming a cross. To end the stitch, go down through the fabric to the wrong side at D.

French knot

A favourite stitch of embroiderers, the French knot can be used as an individual element, like an eye, scattered about randomly or used to fill in an entire area to create texture. The basic French knot is wrapped once, but you can wrap it twice, three or even four times to create a larger knot.

1 Bring the needle up at A and twist through the thread by bringing it over the needle.

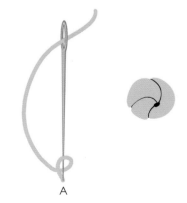

2 Pull the needle up over the thread and back down into A.

Chain stitch

Chain stitch is one of the most versatile stitches. It's basically a series, or chain, of loops. It can be used as an outline or filler. Single chain stitches are often used individually or to make flower petals, called lazy daisy. Zigzag chain stitch uses chain stitches worked at an angle to create a zigzag effect.

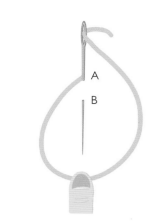

1 Bring needle through fabric at A. Form a loop and hold down with your thumb or finger. Insert the needle at A again and come back through the fabric at B. Gently pull the thread through to form the first chain.

2 Repeat step one, always inserting the needle where the thread came out, drawing it through tightly enough to lay flat, but not so tight that the fabric puckers.

Single chain

Follow step one for chain stitch (see above). Go down through the fabric at C, tacking the top of the stitch down. To end stitch, go down to the wrong side of the fabric at C. Fasten off.

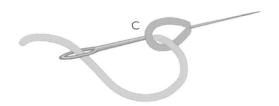

Lazy daisy

Follow steps one and two for single chain (see above). Bring the needle back through the fabric next to the base of the first petal to form the next petal.

Blanket stitch

This is a fun and versatile stitch that instantly adds a finished, vintage look to a piece. Stitches can be made close together for a solid look or spaced out for a more open effect. You can use blanket stitch in the middle or on the edge of a fabric.

1 Bring the thread up at A. Insert the needle in at B and back out at C, holding the thread under the needle. Draw through.

2 Repeat step one, spacing the stitches evenly.

3 To end the stitch, go down through the fabric to the wrong side at C. To work a curved or round shape, work stitches evenly around the edge, opening up the space between the stitches.

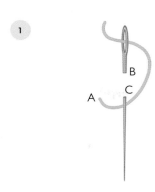

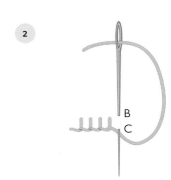

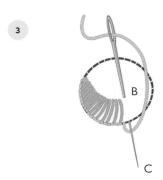

Turning through and finishing

Many of the projects need to be turned through at the end of construction. Before you turn through, trim off any excess fabric by cutting off a triangle across the corners. Carefully clip any curved seam allowances to allow them to flatten. To achieve a professional finish it is important to push out any corners or points so that they are crisp and flat and then press well. There are various tools to help with this but I find a wooden chopstick to be the most useful in getting right into the corner. Just remember not to force it as you may rip the corner seam!

After turning through a project, the gap will always need stitching closed. This can be done in two ways, either by hand stitching with a hemming stitch or by simply placing the folded edges together and top stitching close to the fold on the sewing machine.

PROJECTS

flower brooch

Quick to make, this fabulous flower brooch adds a touch of glamour to a top or jacket. Denim and a contrast fabric are bonded together, the flower design is stitched onto the denim and the brooch is finished with a recycled button and a brooch pin.

SIZE
3½ × 3½in (8.9 × 8.9cm)

YOU WILL NEED
Denim
One 4in (10cm) square

Additional fabrics
One 4in (10cm) square mustard contrast fabric
One 2in (5cm) square mustard felt

Haberdashery
One 4in (10cm) square fusible webbing
One cream button
One 1in (2.5cm) brooch pin
Cream thread
Scissors, needle, pins
Marking pencil

Templates
Flower template (page 131)

PREPARATION
The small square of denim needed for this project can be cut from any item of denim clothing that does not contain a seam or surface stitching.

1 Fuse the denim, fusible webbing and mustard squares together following the manufacturer's guidance so that the right side of the denim is facing upwards and the right side of the mustard fabric is facing downwards.

2 Trace the flower template onto paper, cut out and pin the template to the fused square. Cut out the flower shape carefully. Mark a dot in the middle of the flower. Using the cream thread and starting on the marked dot, stitch out to and around each petal, stitching ¼in (6mm) in from the outer edge. Stitch back to the middle each time.

3 Stitch the button to the middle of the flower.

4 Cut an oval shape from the felt square and using over stitches through the small holes, stitch the brooch pin to the middle of the oval.

5 Stitch the felt oval to the back of the brooch using small slip stitches (page 22).

6 Press the brooch gently around the petal edges with the iron.

tips

• Match the thread for stitching and the button to a coat or jacket for a coordinated look.

• Substitute the button for a fabric yoyo. They are simple to make and you can find instructions on the Internet.

decorative cuff

Pair your denim clothing with a stylish decorative cuff. This versatile cuff can be opened and closed and worn in two different ways. Making good use of the waistband on a pair of jeans, the cuff is embellished with embroidery stitches.

SIZE
10½ × 1½in (26.7 × 3.8cm) flat

YOU WILL NEED
Denim
Two 5½ × 1½in (14 × 3.8cm) sections of waistband,
one containing the button and the other the buttonhole

Additional fabrics
One 4in (10cm) square mustard contrast fabric
One 2in (5cm) square mustard felt

Haberdashery
Navy thread for piecing
Gold embroidery thread
Scissors, needle, pins, ruler

PREPARATION
The denim needed for this project is from a section of waistband cut from the front of a pair of jeans. Both sides of the waistband, including the button and buttonhole, are used. Carefully cut the waistband away from the jeans, cutting as close as possible to the seam line.

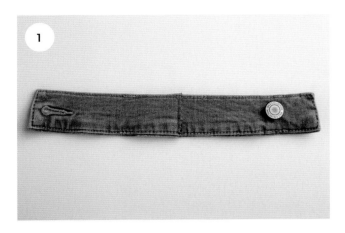

1 To stitch the cuff together, take both sections of the waistband and overlap the raw edges by ¼in (6mm) so that one section is on top of the other. Pin in place, then stitch up and down, through all the layers, at least three times to secure.

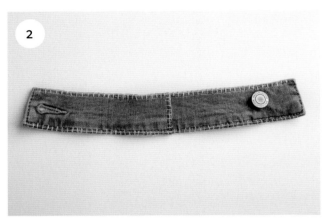

2 Using the gold embroidery thread and a blanket stitch (page 25), stitch over the seam that was stitched in step one. Continue to blanket stitch along each long edge of the cuff, stopping ½in (13mm) from each end.

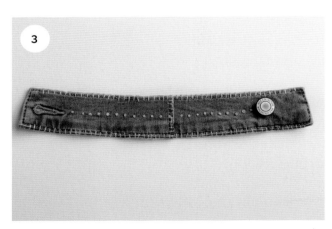

3 Using the gold embroidery thread, stitch a row of French knots (page 23) horizontally along the middle of the cuff, starting at the end of the buttonhole and finishing by the button. Press well.

tips

• The cuff may be worn in two different ways; each side of the band can be placed directly on top of the other or the ends of the bands can be angled.

• Replace the French knots with embroidered flowers for an alternative look.

phone case

A robust and hard-wearing storage case for your mobile phone. The great thing is that the small pockets on the front are perfect for keys and cards so everything is kept securely in one place. A very quick make, the denim pocket is folded, stitched, refolded and stitched again to create the phone case.

SIZE
4½ × 7½in (11.4 × 19cm)

YOU WILL NEED
Denim
9½ × 8in (24 × 20.5cm) front jeans pocket

Haberdashery
Navy thread for piecing
2in (5cm) black hook and loop sew-in tape
Scissors, needle, pins, ruler

PREPARATION
One front pocket cut from a pair of jeans is needed for this project. You may need to remove a belt loop if it is where the raw edges meet as it will be too thick to stitch in the seam.

1 With right sides together and the waistband at the top, fold the 9½ × 8in (24 × 20.5cm) pocket in half and stitch down the side with a double row of stitching.

2 Refold the pocket that has been stitched in step one so that the seam is in the middle at the back. Pin in place and stitch across the bottom edge with a double row of stitching. You may find that the pocket lining is larger than the denim but it is important to stitch all the way across this as well.

3 Take the hook and loop tape and position one piece of the tape on the wrong side of the front of the case in the middle, ¼in (6mm) from the top. Using a slip stitch (page 22), stitch the tape to the denim. Align the second piece of tape on the back of the case and stitch in place.

4 Turn the phone case through so that it is right side out. Press well.

coin pouch

A handy little pouch for coins with a detachable key ring; great for keeping those small essential items securely together. The pouch is constructed from a single piece of denim with a robust metal zip in the centre and finished with a key ring on a piece of recycled denim seam.

SIZE
4¼ × 4¼in (10.8 × 10.8cm)

YOU WILL NEED
Denim
One 5 × 9in (12.7 × 23cm) rectangle
One 4in (10cm) strip of seam

Haberdashery
One 4in (10cm) beige metal zip
One key ring
Navy thread for piecing
Scissors, needle, pins

PREPARATION
The denim needed for this project can be cut from any item of denim clothing that does not contain any surface stitching. The strip of denim for the key ring is simply a thick seam cut from the side seam of a pair of jeans.

1 Take the 5 × 9in (12.7 × 23cm) denim rectangle and on each of the 5in (12.7cm) sides, press under ½in (1.3cm) towards the wrong side of the fabric.

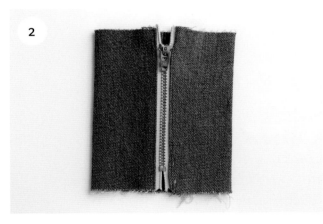

2 Take the zip and pin it to one of the folded fabric edges so that the folded edge is ¼in (6mm) away from the metal teeth of the zip. Top stitch in place using the navy thread. Open the zip and repeat, stitching the second side of the zip to the second folded fabric edge.

3 To stitch the key ring, take the 4in (10cm) strip of seam, thread the ring onto the strip and fold in half, placing the raw ends of the seams next to each other and not on top of each other. Stitch ⅛in (3mm) away from the raw edge across both ends.

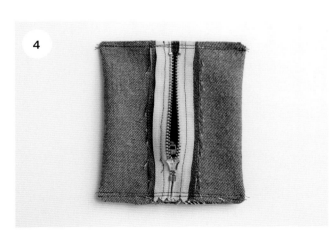

4 Turn the unit completed in step two inside out so that the right sides of the fabrics are facing each other, ensuring that the zip is flat in the middle and pin across each end. Slip the key ring on the seam into the pinned seam that is opposite the zip pull, ensuring that the raw ends of the seam are in line with the seam to be stitched. Stitch twice across this seam. Open the zip and then stitch the seam twice on the opposite end.

5 Turn the pouch right-side out. Push out the corners and press.

tips

• To hold the zip in place before stitching, a little fabric glue can be used.

• A matching zip pull charm and key ring would make the little pouch very stylish.

zippy pouch

Little pouches are so handy for everyday use. Slip one into your handbag or work bag to store small items and keep everything neat and tidy. The really good thing about a pouch made in denim is that it will withstand daily wear and tear. The outer pouch has a contrast fabric stripe across the middle, a shaped base and is quilted. The pouch is lined with cotton fabric and finished with a zip.

SIZE
8 × 7½in (20.3 × 19cm)

YOU WILL NEED
Denim
Two 8½ × 3½in (21.6 × 8.9cm) rectangles
Two 8½ × 4½in (21.6 × 11.4cm) rectangles

Additional fabrics
Two 8½ × 2½in (21.6 × 6.3cm) rectangles mustard print
Two 8½ × 9¼in (21.6 × 23.5cm) rectangles mustard print

Haberdashery
Two 8½ × 9½in (21.6 × 24cm) rectangles fusible wadding
One 8in (20.3cm) zip
5in (12.7cm) mustard ribbon ¼in (6mm) wide
Gold thread for piecing and quilting
Scissors, pins, ruler, marking pencil

PREPARATION
Small pieces of denim are needed for this project so they can be cut from any item of denim clothing.

1 Stitch an 8½ × 3½in (21.6 × 8.9cm) denim rectangle to the top of an 8½ × 2½in (21.6 × 6.3cm) mustard rectangle. Stitch an 8½ × 4½in (21.6 × 11.4cm) denim rectangle to the bottom of the mustard rectangle. Press the seams open. Repeat with the second set of fabrics.

2 Iron the fusible wadding to the wrong side of each outer pouch unit completed in step one. Machine quilt each of the outer pouch units by stitching diagonal lines across the pouch in both directions. Space them out 2in (5cm) apart, symmetrically on the piece.

3 To attach the zip, place the first outer pouch unit right side up and place the zip face down on the front of it, matching the top edge. Pin in place and then pin the 8½ × 9¼in (21.6 × 23.5cm) mustard rectangle on top, right side down. Stitch along the top edge to secure the lining, zip and outer pouch. Repeat to attach the zip to the second pouch unit.

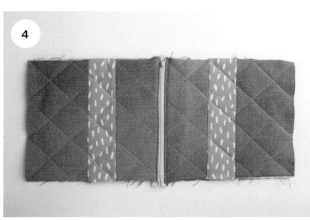

4 Open out each unit and press. Stitch along the top edge ⅛in (3mm) each side of the zip.

5 Open the zip halfway and place the two outer pouch units right sides together, with the lining units also right sides together. Pin and stitch all the way around the edge, leaving a 3in (7.5cm) gap in stitching in the bottom of the lining.

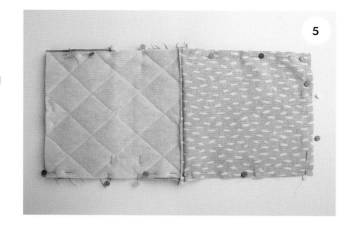

6 To shape the base, match the middle seam of the base with the side seam. Measure 1¼in (3.2cm) along the side seam and stitch across. Cut off the excess fabric. Repeat on the other corner and then on both corners of the lining.

7 Turn the pouch through the opening in the lining so it is right side out. Slip stitch (page 22) the opening closed. Press well, then tie the ribbon on the zip pull.

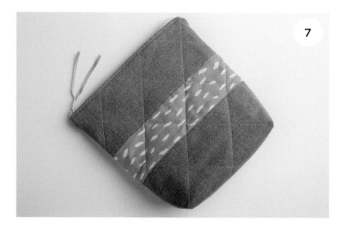

tips

• When stitching the outer units and the lining units together, it makes a difference if the teeth of the zip point towards the lining fabric. This makes the part of the pouch where the zip meets the side seams look much neater.

• It is very important that you remember to open the zip halfway in step five. If you forget, then you will be unable to turn the pouch out to the right side.

water bottle carrier

Your water bottle will never be too far away with this handy bottle carrier, perfect for using when you are out and about. The sturdy strap means you can carry the bottle over your shoulder and the handy pocket on the front is ideal for storing small items. The carrier is finished with a little decorative trim.

SIZE
6 × 11½in (15.2 × 29cm) excluding handle

YOU WILL NEED
Denim
One 12½ × 13in (31.8 × 33cm) rectangle including
the pocket in the middle
One 2½ × 24in (6.3 × 61cm) strip

Haberdashery
28in (71.1cm) beige tape ½in (13mm) wide
Two rectangular buttons
One heart-shaped button
Beige and navy thread for piecing
Beige embroidery thread
Scissors, needle, pins
Marking pencil

PREPARATION
The denim needed for this project can be cut from the top back section of a pair of jeans and include the pocket. When selecting the denim, try to position the pocket in the middle of the cut rectangle and include the finished waistband. An extra strip of denim will be needed for the strap and this can be cut from the leg section. Strips can be cut and joined to get the required length.

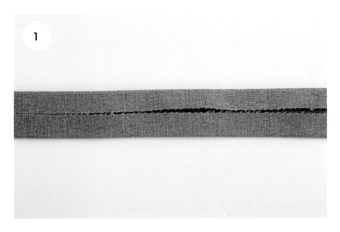

1 To stitch the strap, take the 2½ × 24in (6.3 × 61cm) denim strip and fold each long edge to the middle of the strip so that the right side of the fabric is facing upwards. Press well.

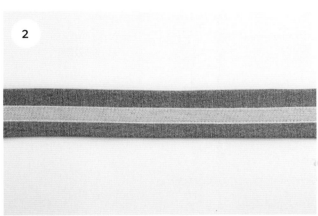

2 Cut the beige tape to measure 24in (61cm) and place this over the raw edges of the denim strap, ensuring that the raw edges are covered by the tape and the tape is positioned in the middle of the denim. Using the beige thread, top stitch the tape to the denim, stitching down each side.

3 To attach the strap, take the 12½ × 13in (31.8 × 33cm) denim rectangle and measure 3in (7.6cm) in from each outer edge, along the waistband. Pin the strap in place so that ½in (13mm) of each end of the strap is below the waistband on the inside of the fabric. Stitch the strap in place by stitching around the ½in (13mm) section twice with the navy thread.

4 With right sides together, take the unit completed in step three, fold in half so that the waistband is at the top, ensure that the strap is out of the way and stitch down the side and across the bottom. Neaten the seam with a row of zigzag stitching.

5 To shape the base of the carrier, match the bottom seam line with the back seam on one side and, on the second side, match the bottom seam with the mid-point on the front of the carrier. On each side, measure in 1in (2.5cm) from the end corner of the seam line and draw a line across from edge to edge. Stitch on the drawn line. Turn right side out and press well.

6 Using the beige embroidery thread and a running stitch (page 22), stitch the remaining 4in (10cm) strip of beige tape to the pocket, positioning the tape 2in (5cm) from the top edge of the pocket and stitching along each outer edge of tape. Make sure that you are only stitching through the pocket and not through the body of the carrier. Stitch a rectangular button to each end of the tape and the heart button in the middle.

tips

• The measurements of the carrier could be changed to fit an exact bottle size if you have a favourite water bottle.

• The decorative trim could be left off for a plain but stylish finish.

tote bag

A large, roomy bag with handy pockets, this is perfect for shopping or days out. Using the top of a pair of jeans, this tote has ready-made pockets on both the back and front of the bag. It is finished with some strong leather handles and fabric trim. The tote has a removable inner base which can be taken out before washing.

SIZE
14½ × 13 × 3½in (36.8 × 33 × 8.9cm)

YOU WILL NEED
Denim
The top section of one pair of jeans. Measure 6in (15.2cm) down from the crotch and cut off both legs
One 4 × 14in (10 × 35.6cm) rectangle

Additional fabrics
3in (7.6cm) wide beige/rust print cut across width of fabric

Haberdashery
One 3 × 13in (7.6 × 33cm) piece of card, thick plastic or similar
24in (61cm) beige bag handles
Beige and navy thread for piecing
Navy embroidery thread
Glue stick
Scissors, needle, pins, ruler, marking pencil

PREPARATION
The denim for this project comes from the top of a pair of jeans with the legs cut off. The size of the bag will be dependent on the size of the jeans but the measurements and the instructions will be the same.

1 Take the top section of the jeans and cut up the seam line of the inner leg and crotch section to open out. Refold the jeans so that the side seams are on top of each other in the middle. Working first on the zip side, use the marking pencil to rule a straight line from the point where the zip finishes to the bottom raw edge at a right angle to the raw edge. Pin. Repeat on the opposite side on the back seam.

2 Stitch on the drawn lines. Cut away the excess fabric and then sew a parallel row of stitches ⅛in (3mm) away from the first line.

3 Refold the jeans top section so that the zip is back in the middle. With right sides facing, pin the bottom raw edges together and stitch, then stitch a parallel row of stitching ⅛in (3mm) away from the first line of stitching.

4 To shape the bottom of the bag, match the bottom seam line with the side seams on each side and measure in 1½in (3.8cm) from the end corner of the seam line. Draw a line across from edge to edge using the marking pencil. Stitch on the drawn line and then stitch a parallel row of stitching ⅛in (3mm) away from the first line of stitching. Cut off the excess fabric. Turn right side out and press well.

5 To make the bag base, take the 3 × 13in (7.6 × 33cm) piece of card and the 4 × 14in (10 × 35.6cm) denim rectangle. Glue the wrong side of the denim to the card, leaving ½in (13mm) of denim around all sides. Fold the remaining edges of denim on to the card, glue down, then leave to dry. Place the bag base in the bottom of the bag.

6 To make the fabric trim, take the 3in (7.6cm) fabric strip and press under ¼in (6mm) on one long edge. On the opposite edge press under ½in (13mm). Fold the ¼in (6mm) edge on top of the opposite folded edge so that it overlaps by ¼in (6mm). Fold under the remaining raw ends. Pin in place, then use the beige thread to top stitch close to the folded edges. Press.

7 Using the navy embroidery thread and a backstitch (page 22), stitch the handles to the bag so that they are evenly positioned on the bag front and back. Thread the fabric trim through the belt loops and tie in place.

tips

• Fabric handles could be substituted for the purchased handles if you prefer and could be cut from the leftover jeans legs.

• Instead of making a contrast fabric trim, a thin silk or chiffon scarf could be threaded through the belt loops.

messenger bag

- -

A great bag to use when out and about, this is perfect for all those essential items that are carried around every day. The bag is fully lined with a contrast fabric, has a pocket on the front, an inner magnetic snap for security and is finished with a cross body strap.

SIZE
11 × 12½in (27.9 × 31.8cm) excluding strap

YOU WILL NEED
Denim
One 11½ × 25in (29 × 63.5cm) rectangle with the top of a pocket
about 5½in (14cm) from one 11½in (29cm) end. Pieces of denim can
be joined to get a rectangle of this size
One 3¼ × 32in (8.2 × 81.2cm) strip
One 3 × 13in (7.6 × 33cm) strip

Additional fabrics
One 11½ × 24½in (29 × 62.2cm) rectangle beige print

Haberdashery
11½ × 25in (29 × 63.5cm) medium-weight fusible interfacing
Two 1in (2.5cm) squares medium-weight fusible interfacing
Two 1½in (3.8cm) metal D rings
One magnetic snap
Blue thread for piecing
Scissors, pins, ruler, marking pencil

PREPARATION
The denim for this project came from a skirt. I chose to use a
skirt as there was a lot of flat denim in the garment but any large
pieces would be suitable, just ensure that there are no thick
seams close to the bag top.

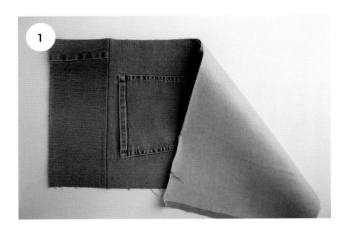

1 To stitch the outer bag, take the 11½ × 25in (29 × 63.5cm) denim rectangle and iron the 11½ × 25in (29 × 63.5cm) fusible interfacing rectangle to the wrong side of the denim.

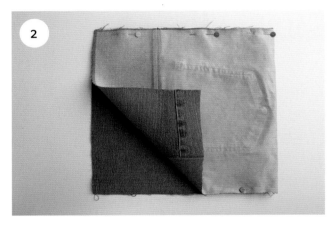

2 Fold the outer bag unit in half with right sides facing and stitch down each side. Clip the corners and turn the bag right side out.

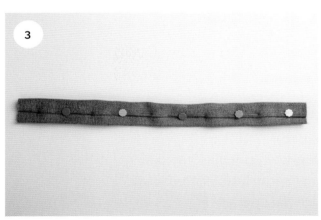

3 To stitch the strap loops, take the 3 × 13in (7.5 × 33cm) denim strip and press under ¼in (6mm) on one long side. Fold the raw edge of the strip to the middle so that the wrong sides are facing and then the folded edge on top. The folded edge should overlap the raw edge. Pin in place and top stitch down the folded edge.

4 Cut the unit made in step three in half to make two loops. Insert each strap loop into a D ring. Fold the loop in half, making sure that the raw edges are even. Stitch across the fabric ½in (13mm) away from the D ring.

5 Pin a strap loop to the front and back of the outer bag on diagonally opposite corners, 1½in (3.8cm) in from the side seams. Stitch in place with an ⅛in (3mm) seam.

6 To add the snap, mark both ends of the lining 1in (2.5cm) down from the 11½in (29cm) edge and 5¾in (14.6cm) in from each side. Iron the 1in (2.5cm) squares of interfacing to the wrong side over the marked dots. Make two small holes either side of the dots, insert the prongs from the right side, add the back plates and press flat. Fold right sides facing with the 11½in (29cm) edges at the top together. Stitch down each side leaving a 4in (10cm) gap in one side.

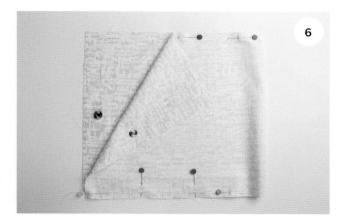

7 Slide the outer bag inside the lining so that the right sides of the fabric are facing and the side seams match. Keeping the strap loops firmly tucked down, pin the top edges together, then stitch around the top edge of the bag. Turn through the opening and stitch the gap in the lining closed. Carefully press the top of the bag so that the lining matches the top edge of the outer bag, then top stitch around the edge.

8 To stitch the strap, take the 3¼ × 32in (8.2 × 81.3cm) denim strip and fold the long raw edges to the middle of the strip so that the wrong sides of the fabric are facing. Fold in half so that the folded edges lie on top of each other and top stitch down each side. Press.

9 To add the strap, thread the ends through the D rings on the strap loops and pin each end back on itself 1½in (3.8cm) up from the ring. Stitch across the strap several times for extra strength. Press well.

tips

• If you are stitching pieces of denim together to make the rectangle needed for this project, you may wish to have a pocket on both sides of the bag.

• The length of the strap could be made longer or shorter to suit the height of the user.

storage baskets

These baskets will look pretty on your shelves as well as being extremely useful for storing cosmetics, stationery, small toys or sewing supplies. The baskets are lined with a contrast fabric and can be made in whatever sizes you like, depending on the width of the denim.

SIZE
6 × 8½in (15.2 × 21.6cm)

YOU WILL NEED

Denim
One 9 × 10in (23 × 25cm) jeans leg – the 9in (23cm) measurement is one side of the folded leg, but both sides are needed for this project therefore the leg needs to be 18in (45.7cm) in circumference

Additional fabrics
One 18½ × 12in (47 × 30.5cm) contrast fabric

Haberdashery
One 18½ × 12in (47 × 30.5cm) rectangle medium-weight fusible interfacing
Navy and grey thread for piecing
Scissors, needle, pins
Marking pencil

PREPARATION
These baskets are made from the straight leg of a pair of jeans so the width of the basket is determined by the width of the jeans leg. This project will not work with a tapered leg. Cut the bottom hem from one leg and measure upwards. The measurements given in this project will make the basket with grey lining.

1 Turn the 9 × 10in (23 × 25cm) jeans leg inside out and carefully iron the 18½ × 12in (47 × 30.5cm) rectangle of medium-weight fusible interfacing to the wrong side of the leg.

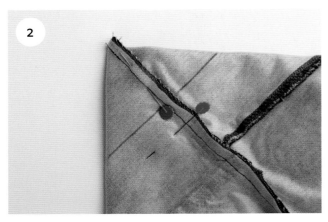

2 With right sides together, stitch across the bottom of the jeans leg. To shape the base, match the bottom seam line with the side seams. On each side, measure in 2in (5cm) from the end corner of the bottom seam line, then draw a line across from edge to edge. Stitch on the drawn line. Cut off the excess fabric.

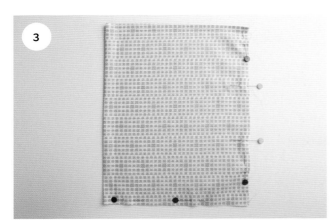

3 To stitch the inner basket, take the 18½ × 12in (47 × 30.5cm) grey rectangle and fold it in half, right sides facing, with the 18½in (47cm) opening at the top. Pin and stitch down the side and across the bottom, leaving a 2½in (6.3cm) opening in the side seam. To shape the inner base, repeat the instructions in step two.

4 Turn the outer basket through and place inside the inner basket so that right sides are facing and the shaped bases line up with each other. Pin around the top.

5 Stitch all the way round the top. Turn the basket through the gap in the stitching. Push out the corners and slip stitch (page 22) the gap closed. Pull the lining 1in (2.5cm) up from the top of the outer basket and pin in place. Carefully stitch in the seam line, where the lining meets the denim, to secure the denim and the lining together. Press well.

5

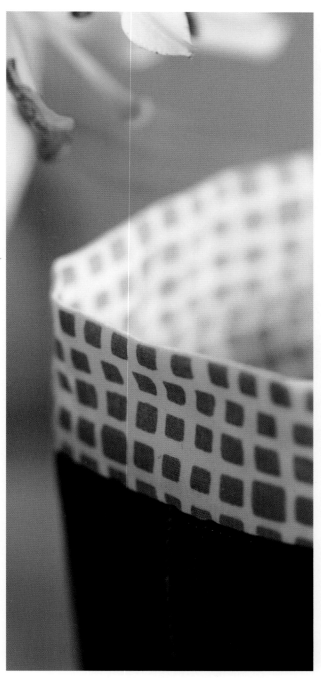

tips

• A Teflon sheet is invaluable when ironing the interfacing to the denim. Use it on top of the interfacing and the iron will never stick to it.

• Different-sized storage baskets can be stitched from the varying sized jean legs, just adjust the size of the lining to match. You will have a number of different sized storage baskets in no time at all.

drawstring bag

This handy and robust drawstring bag has a multitude of uses like storing toys, shoes, school books, clothing and so much more. The drawstring allows the bag to be hung neatly out of the way when not in use. The exterior of the bag is made from patched and stitched together pieces of denim while the lining is a cotton print.

SIZE
12 × 15in (30.5 × 38.4cm)

YOU WILL NEED
Denim
Two pockets with at least 1in (2.5cm) denim around each side and lots of scraps

Additional fabrics
Two 12½ × 15½in (31.8 × 39.4cm) contrast fabrics

Haberdashery
72in (183cm) white cord ¼in (6mm) wide
Grey thread for piecing
Safety pin for threading
Scissors, pins, ruler, marking pencil

PREPARATION
This is a great project for scraps of denim and if you have made some of the other projects in the book you will have accumulated a few! I have started each side of the bag by cutting a front or back pocket from a pair of jeans and then constructing the panels by adding pieces and strips of denim.

1 To add an exterior panel, stitch a strip of denim to the bottom of one pocket. Press the seams open. Stitch a same-length piece to one side of the pocket, then to the other. Continue adding strips of denim, trimming and straightening edges and pressing seams open as you go. Include some of the features, such as double-stitched exterior seams, until the panel measures 12½ × 15½in (31.8 × 39.4cm).

2 To stitch the second exterior panel, repeat step one with a second pocket and denim scraps. Press both pieces well.

3 To stitch the outer bag together, take both units completed in steps one and two and measure and mark 1in (2.5cm) and 2in (5cm) down from the top of the outer edge on both sides. Place the panels right sides together and pin each side and across the bottom, leaving a gap between the markings. Stitch down each side and across the bottom, stopping the stitching between the markings. Press seams open and clip corners. Turn through.

4 To stitch the lining, pin the two 12½ × 15½in (31.8 × 39.4cm) contrast fabric rectangles right sides together and stitch down each side and across the bottom, leaving a 5in (12.7cm) gap for turning in the bottom. Trim the corners. Place the outer bag inside the lining, right sides together, and pin all the way round the top edge. Sew around the edge, matching the side seams. Neaten the seam with a row of zigzag stitching.

5 Turn the bag through the gap in the lining. Push out the corners and slip stitch (page 22) the gap closed. Press and top stitch around the top edge ⅛in (3mm) away from the top. To stitch the casing for the drawstrings, measure 1¾in (4.4cm) down from the top of the bag and 1in (2.5cm) above this and draw two horizontal lines on both sides using a marking pencil to align with the gaps left in the bag seams. Stitch across both of these drawn lines.

6 Take the 72in (183cm) white cord and cut in half. To insert the drawstrings in the casing, attach the safety pin to one end of one length of cord. Starting on the right-hand side, thread the end of the cord with the safety pin through the front casing, back through the back casing and tie the ends in a knot on the right side. Repeat the process with the second length of cord, but this time start on the left-hand side.

tip

• I have stitched my bag in grey denim scraps but it would look fabulous in denim scraps of many different colours to give it a patchwork effect.

notebook cover

Turn a plain notebook into a treasured possession with this sparkly cover. The beauty of making your own cover is that, once the book is full of notes and lists, you can simply take off the cover and re-use it on your next notebook. The notebook cover is constructed from several pieces of denim, a pocket cut from a pair of jeans, and flaps at each side to tuck around the notebook.

SIZE
6¼ × 8¼in (15.9 × 21cm)

YOU WILL NEED
Denim
One 6½in (16.5cm) square pocket (the pocket will need at least
½in/13mm of denim around the pocket)
Two 6½ × 2in (16.5 × 5cm) strips
Three 7½ × 9½in (19 × 24cm) rectangles

Additional fabrics
One 13½ × 9½in (34.3 × 24cm) beige floral print rectangle

Haberdashery
One 13½ × 9½in (34.3 × 24cm) rectangle medium-weight
fusible interfacing
Navy thread for piecing
Cream embroidery thread
Scissors, needle, pins
One 6 × 8in (15.2 × 20.3cm) notebook

PREPARATION
The focal point of the notebook is the sparkly trim on the pocket
so if you are able to cut a back pocket with some existing sparkly
embellishment from a piece of denim clothing it will work well with
this project. The other pieces of denim needed can be cut from
the leg of a pair of jeans or any other denim item and may contain
seams or top stitching.

1 Using the cream embroidery thread, stitch a small flower to the pocket using lazy daisy stitch (page 24) for the flower and backstitch (page 22) for the stem. Ensure that the stitches only go through the outer pocket.

2 Take the two 6½ × 2in (16.5 × 5cm) denim strips and stitch one above the pocket and the other below. Press the seams open. Take one of the 7½ × 9½in (19 × 24cm) denim rectangles and stitch it to the left side of the pocket. Press the seams open.

3 Iron the fusible interfacing to the reverse of the unit completed in step two. To make the inner flaps, fold each of the remaining 7½ × 9½in (19 × 24cm) denim rectangles in half vertically, wrong sides together, and press. Place an inner flap on each end of the right side of the notebook cover so that the raw edges line up and the folded edge faces the middle.

4 Lay the 13½ × 9½in (34.3 × 24cm) beige floral print rectangle on top of the cover, right sides together. Pin around the outer edge, then stitch around all four sides, leaving a 3in (7.6cm) gap in stitching on one long side.

5 Trim the corners and turn the cover through the gap so it is right side out. Push out the corners and press well. Close the opening with small, neat slip stitches (page 22) and add your notebook.

5

tips

• To personalize the notebook cover, instead of adding an embroidered flower, stitch the recipient's name using backstitch.

• The inner flaps could also be embellished with embroidery for a special touch.

luggage tags

- -

The perfect gift for the traveller. Robust and hard-wearing; these luggage tags will last for many years. The luggage tags have a denim front and back and are stabilized inside with interfacing. They have a perfect-sized window of strong, clear plastic so you can write a label with all your travel information and slip it safely inside. The tags are finished with a denim strap.

SIZE
6 × 3½in (15.2 x 8.9cm) excluding strap

YOU WILL NEED
Denim
Four 6 × 3½in (15.2 × 8.9cm) rectangles
Two double-folded hems, cut from legs of jeans
(these need to be cut so that they are circular)

Haberdashery
Four 6 × 3½in (15.2 × 8.9cm) rectangles medium-weight fusible interfacing
Two 4 × 3in (10 × 7.6cm) rectangles clear plastic
or acetate or similar
Black thread for piecing
Scissors, pins, ruler, marking pencil

PREPARATION
The fabric quantities in this pattern will make two luggage tags.
It only requires small pieces of denim so they can be cut from any
item of denim clothing. Two hems cut from the legs of jeans will
also be required.

1 Take two 6 × 3½in (15.2 x 8.9cm) denim rectangles and carefully iron a 6 × 3½in (15.2 × 8.9cm) rectangle of medium-weight fusible interfacing to the wrong side of each denim rectangle.

2 To shape the top of the tag, take both of the units completed in step one and measure 1in (2.5cm) in from each corner along one 3½in (8.9cm) edge and 1in (2.5cm) in from each corner along the corresponding 6in (15.2cm) edges. Mark and draw a line on the diagonal from mark to mark. Cut along the lines.

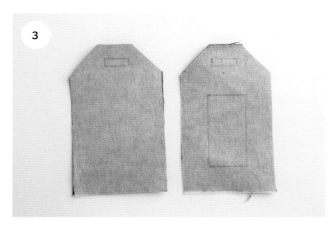

3 To make the window, on one of the tags completed in step two, draw a 3 × 2in (7.5 × 5cm) rectangle in the middle and a small ¼ × ¾in (6 × 19mm) rectangle at the top in the shaped section. On the second tag draw a small rectangle only in exactly the same position as that on the first tag.

4 Cut away the middles of the large and small rectangles and stitch ⅛in (3mm) away from the edges around all inner rectangles. Stitch around each edge twice.

5 With wrong sides together, align both the front and the back tags and stitch down one long side, across the bottom and up the other long side with an ⅛in (3mm) seam. Stitch around each edge twice.

6 Slip the 4 × 3in (10 × 7.6cm) plastic rectangle inside the tag. Take one circular denim hem and pull it through the small rectangle and back through itself creating a secure loop. To stitch the second luggage tag repeat all steps using the second set of materials.

tips

• The measurements for these tags can easily be altered to create smaller or larger tags in order to fit specific sized luggage.

• The circular hems used in the straps could also be replaced with strips of denim.

shorts

- -

Turn a favourite pair of jeans into some shorts that are embellished with creativity and pizzazz. They will be truly individual and no one else will have a pair the same. Cut down a pair of jeans into some shorts and customize them with hand stitching and simple embroidery. The legs are finished with frayed edges.

SIZE
Any size

YOU WILL NEED
Denim
One pair of jeans

Haberdashery
White, pink and maroon embroidery threads
Scissors, needle, pins, ruler, marking pencil

PREPARATION
Choose a pair of jeans that fit well but perhaps are worn around the bottom of the legs. Put the jeans on and mark both front and back where you would like the bottom of the legs on the shorts to be. It is very tempting to cut them too short as they will look longer when laid flat, so don't cut shorter than your mark. You will also lose a bit of length in fraying the edges. If in doubt, cut them longer, then try them on again. Identify any areas that are worn as these are ideal for embellishment. I have identified two worn areas on the front of these jeans.

1 Cut the legs off the jeans at the marked measurement. Ensure that the edges are straight.

2 Draw a rectangle around any worn areas with the marking pencil. Using a running stitch (page 22) and the white embroidery thread, stitch around the rectangle. Then stitch again two more times inside the rectangle, leaving a ¼in (6mm) space between each line of stitching. Using the maroon embroidery thread, stitch two small flowers using a lazy daisy stitch (page 24) above the stitched rectangle.

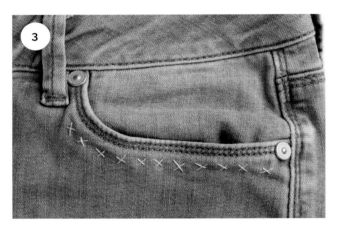

3 Using the pink embroidery thread, stitch a row of pink crosses (page 23) under the edge of the front pocket seams. Position the crosses ½in (13mm) away from the edge to avoid the bulky seam.

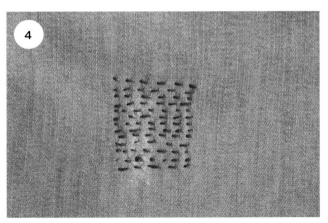

4 Using the maroon embroidery thread, stitch small running stitches horizontally across any worn areas.

5 Using the maroon embroidery thread, stitch a row of horizontal chain stitches (page 24) 1¼in (3.2cm) above the bottom raw edge of each leg.

6 Fray the bottom edges of each leg by pulling the threads away from the fabric. It may be necessary to snip into the edges with tiny cuts to encourage fraying. Press well.

tips

• These shorts have been embellished quite simply and on the front only but further embellishment could be added to the back of the shorts and in greater detail.

• If there are rips in the denim, patches could be stitched on first before embellishing.

• For the great look of a frayed hole in the shorts without the see-through-to-the-skin downside, cut a frayed patch from your original garment, allowing a 2in (5cm) seam allowance, then turn the edges under, pin and top stitch onto the shorts, by hand or machine, as you would a pocket or patch (page 124, step three).

skirt

Turn a favourite pair of jeans into a skirt and embellish with extra patches. Your skirt will be a one-off design – no one else will have one quite the same! Cut apart a pair of jeans and insert some extra denim to provide the additional fullness to make a skirt. Add patches of denim from leftover scraps to stitch on individuality.

SIZE
Any size

YOU WILL NEED
Denim
One pair of jeans
Two large pieces, each will need to be 2in (5cm) larger on each side than the gap left between the legs of the jeans.
One 1¾in (4.4cm) square
One 2½in (6.3cm) square
One 3½in (8.9cm) square
One 1 × 7½in (2.5 × 19cm) strip of flat seam

Haberdashery
Navy thread for piecing
Scissors, pins, ruler, marking pencil

PREPARATION
Choose a pair of jeans that fit well but are perhaps worn around the bottom of the legs. Cut up each inner leg and around the crotch section to open up the jeans. Cut out the thick inner seam so that just the raw edges of the denim remain. Cut off the folded hem from the bottom of each leg. Put on the jeans and then mark where you would like the bottom of the skirt to end. Add an extra 2in (5cm) below this mark and cut off the bottom of the legs.

1 To remove the shaping on the back of the jeans where the middle seam sits below the pockets, fold the excess fabric under the seam line and pin in place. Turn under any raw edges. Try to get this as flat as possible.

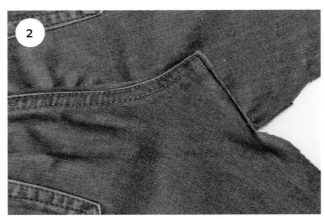

2 Stitch down the seam line so that the excess fabric is folded under the seam. Trim away any excess fabric on the reverse.

3 Working on the front of the jeans, lay one of the large pieces of denim under the gap between the legs. Ensure that the denim lays flat and that it covers the entire space with at least 1in (2.5cm) overlapping the raw edges of the jeans. Turn under ¼in (6mm) on the raw edge of the jeans and pin to the large piece of denim. Repeat for the section on the back with the second large piece of denim.

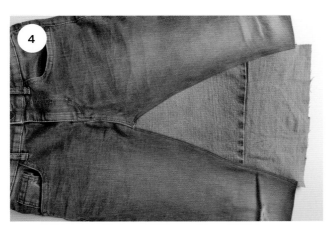

4 Carefully stitch along the turned-under edge of denim, stitching as close as possible to the folded edge all the way around the pinned edges on both sides of the jeans. Turn the skirt inside out and cut away any excess denim from the inserted pieces so that ½in (13mm) remains. Turn right side out and add another line of stitching ¼in (6mm) away from the first line of stitching. Press.

5 To straighten up the bottom of the skirt, trim along the bottom edge so that it is even. Try the skirt on again and check that you are happy with the length. Adjust as necessary. Press under ¼in (6mm) all the way around the hem line. Turn the hem over again by ½in (13mm) and stitch down. Press well.

6 Take the 1¾in (4.4cm), 2½in (6.3cm) and 3½in (8.9cm) squares and pull threads out from each edge to fray. Position the squares on the skirt as desired and stitch twice around each square ¼in (6mm) from the outer edge. Take the 1 × 7½in (2.5 × 19cm) strip of flat seam, position it on the skirt and stitch around the strip twice.

tip

• This skirt has been embellished simply with patches, however you could add many more patches and customize with embroidery.

pendant

This simple, stylish pendant will add a touch of fun to a casual outfit. A perfect child-friendly project involving glue with just a little stitching, the denim strip is coiled around in a swirl and glued in place, beading is added to a covered button in the middle and the pendant is finished with a braid tie.

SIZE
2in (5cm) diameter, excluding tie

YOU WILL NEED
Denim
One 22 × ⅜in (56 × 9mm) strip of seam

Additional fabrics
One 2¼in (5.7cm) square plain cream

Haberdashery
One button ½in (13mm) diameter
Seven gold beads
30in (76.2cm) rust flat braid ¼in (6mm) wide
Cream thread for piecing
Fabric glue
Scissors, needle, ruler, marking pencil

PREPARATION
The denim for this project is a double side seam cut from a pair of jeans.

1 Beginning at one end of the 22 × ⅜in (56 x 9mm) denim strip and leaving a small opening in the middle, wind the strip around in a circular spiral, gluing the strip as you go. Continue until almost the end of the spiral leaving 2in (5cm) unglued. Leave the spiral until the glue has completely dried.

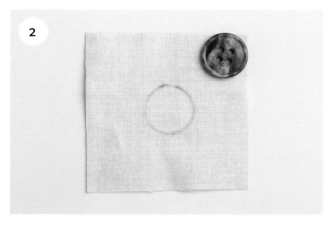

2 Take the 2¼in (5.7cm) cream square and, using the marking pencil, draw around the button on the right side of the fabric in the middle so that you have a marked circle.

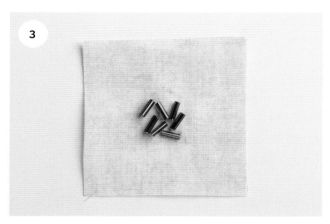

3 Stitch the beads into the marked circle in a random fashion, ensuring that they are all positioned within the circle. Remove the markings.

4 Using the cream thread, stitch a large running stitch (page 22) ½in (13mm) away from the outer edge of the circle of beads. Place the button underneath the stitched beads and inside the circle of stitches and pull up the stitching so that it is gathered tightly and the beads sit on top of the button. Secure the gathering thread and then wind the excess thread around the leftover cream fabric for ¼in (6mm).

5 Add a dab of glue to the middle hole in the spiralled denim and push the fabric through the hole so that the button sits on the top. Trim away any excess fabric on the back.

6 Loop the braid once around the strip of denim spiral that is not glued down and then glue the remaining denim in place. Tie the ends of the braid together.

tip

• There are so many possibilities with this design. The middle could be left empty or a button could be used instead of the beads.

bottle gift bag

There is nothing more thoughtful than giving a bottle of something nice in a handmade gift bag. This gift bag is the perfect size for a bottle of bubbly to celebrate that special occasion.

SIZE
7 × 13in (17.8 × 33cm)

YOU WILL NEED
Denim
One 7 × 15in (17.8 × 38.1cm) jeans leg – the 7in (17.8cm) measurement is one side of the folded leg, however both sides are needed for this project therefore 14in (35.8cm) in circumference
One 4in (10cm) square
One 15in (38.1cm) strip of hem ½in (1.3cm) wide

Haberdashery
15in (38cm) beige rick rack trim ¼in (6mm) wide
15in (38cm) beige tape ½in (13mm) wide
One beige button
Navy and beige threads for piecing
Scissors, needle, pins, ruler

Templates
Flower template (page 131)

PREPARATION
The bottle gift bag is made from the straight leg of a pair of jeans and the width of the bag is dependent on the width of the jeans leg. The project will not work with a tapered leg. Cut the leg from a pair of jeans, measuring from the hem upwards. These jeans did not have a stitched hem so the frayed hem edge will become the top of the bag. Scraps are also needed for the flower and tie.

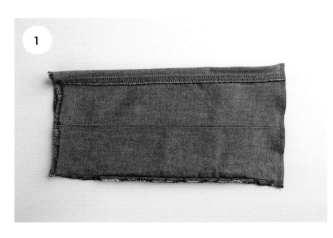

1 Turn the jeans leg inside out and, keeping the side seams at each side, stitch across the bottom raw edge. Stitch across a second time.

2 To shape the bottom of the bag, match the bottom seam line with the side seams. On each side measure in 1½in (4cm) from the end corner of the seam line and draw a line across from edge to edge. Stitch on the drawn line twice, then trim away excess fabric.

3 Turn the bag right side out and stitch the rick rack trim to the top edge. Stitch the beige tape under the rick rack leaving a ¼in (6mm) gap between the two.

4 To make the flower, trace the flower template onto paper, cut out and pin the template to the 4in (10cm) denim square. Cut out the flower shape carefully. Stitch a 1in (2.5cm) wide circle of large running stitches in the middle of the flower and pull up the stitching so that the middle of the flower is gathered. Secure the gathering thread.

5 Stitch the flower to the front of the gift bag approximately halfway down. Stitch the button to the middle of the flower.

6 Pop a bottle into the bag and tie the 15in (38cm) strip of hem around the bag and the neck of the bottle.

tips

• If time is short, there's no need to embellish the gift bag but simply shape the base and add the tie.

• For a coordinated gift, match the trim on the plant pot cover (page 102) with the trim on the bottle gift bag for a stylish combination.

love cushion

Denim paired with navy and pale blue fabrics is always stylish, making this cushion a perfect accompaniment to a squishy sofa. Simple appliquéd letters are stitched to the denim cushion front using raw edge appliqué. The cushion is finished with a contrasting fabric back and stuffed firmly with polyester toy filling.

SIZE
16½ × 13½in (42 × 34.3cm)

YOU WILL NEED
Denim
One 17 × 14in (43.2 × 35.6cm) rectangle

Additional fabrics
One 17 × 14in (43.2 × 35.6cm) rectangle blue fabric
Four 6in (15.2cm) squares blue patterned fabrics
One 3in (7.6cm) square red fabric

Haberdashery
One 10in (25cm) square fusible webbing
Navy and pale grey thread
Polyester toy filling
Scissors, needle, pins

Templates
LOVE letters and small heart templates (pages 130–131)

PREPARATION
The piece of denim needed for this project is quite large so cutting apart one wide leg of a pair of jeans is perfect. The seamed part of the denim sits in the middle of the cushion top.

1 Trace the letters onto the paper side of the fusible webbing. Roughly cut around each traced letter. Place each fusible webbing letter onto the reverse of a 6in (15.2cm) blue square so that the paper side is facing you and iron the letter to the fabric. Cut out each letter neatly on the traced lines.

2 Repeat the above steps with the heart template and the 3in (7.6cm) square of red fabric.

3 Peel the backing paper away from the letters and heart and position them on the 17 × 14in (43.2 × 35.6cm) denim rectangle.

4 Iron in place. Using a straight stitch on the machine and the grey thread, top stitch close to the outer edge of the letters and heart. Stitch around the letters and heart twice.

5 With right sides together, place the appliquéd cushion front on top of the 17 × 14in (43.2 × 35.6cm) blue fabric back. Stitch around each side, leaving a 4in (10cm) gap in the middle of the bottom seam. Trim the corners.

Turn the cushion through the gap so that it is right side out. Push out the corners and press. Stuff firmly with the polyester toy filling. Close the opening with small neat slip stitches (page 22).

5

tips

• Choose the colours and patterns on your letters to match your decor and establish your style – from cool and sophisticated monochrome to bright and jazzy.

• Make a pair of cushions using the same fabrics for the letters in different combinations.

home cushion

A delightful cushion featuring stitchery and buttons that will add a cosy accent to a comfy chair. The letters spelling HOME are stitched on to the cushion top with a variety of techniques including running stitches, buttons and blanket stitched felt. The cushion is finished with a contrasting fabric back, a pompom trim and stuffed firmly with polyester toy filling.

SIZE
18 × 12in (45.7 × 30.5cm)

YOU WILL NEED
Denim
One 18½ × 12½in (47cm × 31.7cm) rectangle

Additional fabrics
One 6in (15.2cm) square white felt
One 18½ × 12½in (47cm × 31.7cm) rectangle navy print

Haberdashery
27 small white buttons
65in (165cm) white pompom trim
Navy thread for piecing
White and pale blue embroidery thread
Polyester toy filling
Scissors, needle, pins, ruler, marking pencil

Templates
Letters H, M, E and heart shape (page 132)

PREPARATION
The denim needed for this project was taken from the leg of a pair of jeans. The leg was cut down the seam line and opened up. As this was not quite wide enough, an extra piece of denim cut from further up the leg was stitched to one end.

1 Trace the letters onto paper and cut out.

2 Pin the M template to the 6in (15.2cm) white felt square, cut out and position on the denim rectangle. Using the marking pencil, trace the H, heart shape and E onto the denim rectangle.

3 Using white embroidery thread and running stitches (page 22), stitch vertically up and down the letter H, leaving an ⅛in (3mm) gap between each row. Repeat for the letter E but this time stitch horizontally. Stitch the small white buttons to the outer edge of the heart shape, ensuring that there are no gaps between buttons. Using the pale blue embroidery thread and a blanket stitch (page 25), stitch the M to the denim.

4 Take the pompom trim and lay it around the edge of the cushion front so that the braid holding the pompoms is on the outer edge and the pompoms are facing in towards the middle. Using an ⅛in (3mm) seam, stitch the braid to the outer edge of the cushion front.

5 With right sides together, place the cushion front on top of the 18½ × 12½in (47cm × 31.7cm) navy print rectangle. Stitch around each side, leaving a 4in (10cm) gap in the middle of the bottom seam. Trim the corners.

6 Turn the cushion through the gap so that it is right side out. Push out the corners and press well. Stuff firmly with the polyester toy filling. Close the opening with small, neat slip stitches (page 22).

tip

• Change up the techniques used for adding the letters to the cushion front, for example by using the buttons to make another letter and changing the stitched letters to felt letters.

plant pot cover

----

*Bring the outdoors inside by adding a lovely plant or some spring bulbs
to this stylish plant pot. It's great for sitting on a window sill or perfect to
give as a gift. A quick and easy make, the denim is stitched into a shaped pot
and the top is turned over and decorated with coordinating trim.*

SIZE
5 × 7in (12.7 × 17.8cm)

YOU WILL NEED
Denim
One 8 × 12in (20.3 × 30.5cm) jeans leg – the 8in
(20.3cm) measurement is one side of the folded leg
but both sides are needed for this project therefore
16in (40.6cm) in circumference
Potted plant

Haberdashery
18in (45.7cm) navy rick rack trim 1¼in (3.2cm) wide
Navy thread for piecing
Scissors, pins, ruler, marking pencil

PREPARATION
The plant pot is made from the straight leg of a pair of jeans
and the width of the pot is dependent on the width of the
jeans leg. This project will not work with a tapered leg. Cut
the leg from a pair of jeans, measuring from the hem upwards.

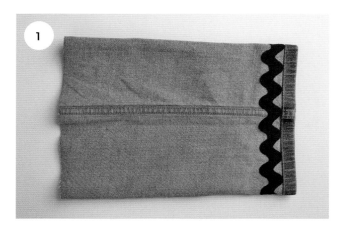

1 Turn the 8 × 12in (20.3 × 30.5cm) jeans leg inside out and stitch the rick rack trim to the hem edge on the wrong side of the fabric, positioning the trim so that it touches the turned-over hem. Where the trim meets and overlaps, fold under the raw edge on the top and pin in place. Stitch the trim to the denim by stitching through the middle and around the top and bottom edges.

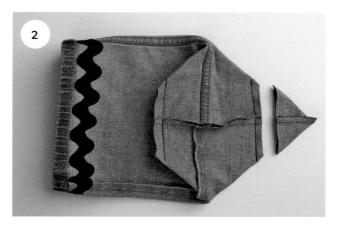

2 To shape the bottom of the pot, place the seam lines of the jeans leg on top of each other and with right sides together, stitch across the bottom raw edge. Match the bottom seam line with the side fold on each side. Measure in 2in (5cm) from the end corner of the seam line, draw a line from edge to edge with the marking pencil. Stitch on the drawn line. Cut off the excess fabric.

3 Turn the pot through to the right side. Press well. Turn the top edge down 2in (5cm) so that the trim is facing outwards and pin in place. Stitch around the folded edge as close to the edge as possible to secure.

tip

• A sheet of plastic, a plastic bag or a plant saucer put in the bottom of the pot before adding the potted plant will provide some protection from damp soil.

hanging hearts

These hanging hearts will brighten up a plain wall, door handle or dresser. Stitch a set of three hanging hearts using denim scraps. The hearts are filled with stuffing to give them a softly padded effect and are finished with a hanging loop.

SIZE
6 × 6in (15.2 × 15.2cm)

YOU WILL NEED
Denim
Six 7in (17.8cm) squares
Three ½ × 8in (13mm × 20.3cm) strips

Haberdashery
Navy thread for piecing
Polyester toy filling
Scissors, needle, pins, marking pencil

Templates
Large heart template (page 133)

PREPARATION
The denim needed for this project can be cut from
any item of denim clothing. Any surface seams, top stitching
or parts of pockets are good to include on the front of the hearts
while the back can be kept plain. These quantities of materials
will make a set of three hearts.

1 Trace the heart template onto paper and cut out. Pin the template to the six 7in (17.8cm) denim squares and cut out the shapes.

2 Take the three ½ × 8in (13mm × 20.3cm) denim strips and fold the strips in half with right sides facing outwards. Pin one to the v section of the front piece of each heart. Stitch in place with an ⅛in (3mm) seam.

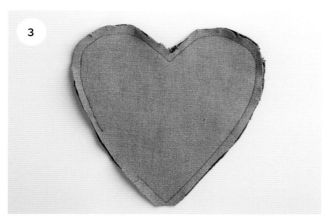

3 With right sides together, place each heart front on top of a heart back. Pin in place. Stitch around each heart, leaving a 2in (5cm) opening in one side. Carefully clip the seams and v section and trim the point.

4 Turn each heart through the gap so that it is right side out. Stuff with the polyester toy filling and close the opening with small, neat slip stitches (page 22).

tooth fairy pillow

The perfect gift for a small child who is waiting for the tooth fairy to visit, the tooth goes in one little pocket and then the treat or a coin comes back in the other. The pillow is just the right size to leave next to the bed overnight in anticipation of a visit. The denim pocket section is bordered by strips of contrasting fabric and decorated with rick rack trim.

SIZE
14½ × 9½in (36.8 × 24cm)

YOU WILL NEED

Denim
One 12 × 7in (30.5 × 17.8cm) rectangle with two pockets

Additional fabrics
Two 12 × 2in (30.5 × 5cm) strips mustard print
Two 10 × 2in (25 × 5cm) strips mustard print
One 15 × 10in (38.1 × 25cm) rectangle mustard print
Two 1½ × 1¾in (3.8 × 4.4cm) motifs mustard print cut with pinking shears

Haberdashery
25in (63.5cm) beige rick rack trim ¼in (6mm) wide
Blue thread for piecing
Cream embroidery thread
Polyester toy filling
Scissors, needle, pins, ruler, pinking shears

PREPARATION
The denim needed for this project was cut from the back of a pair of child's jeans and included both pockets. The pair that I used were for age five.

1 Take the 12 × 7in (30.5 × 17.8cm) denim rectangle and where the shaping occurs at the bottom of the middle seam between the pockets, fold the excess fabric under the seam line and stitch down. Trim away any excess fabric on the reverse.

2 Cut the rick rack trim in half and stitch one piece horizontally across the denim above the pockets and then stitch the second piece of rick rack trim horizontally across the denim below the pockets. Trim away any excess rick rack in line with the outer raw edges.

3 Take the two 12 × 2in (30.5 × 5cm) mustard strips and stitch to the top and bottom of the unit completed in step two. Press the seams away from the middle. Take the two 10 × 2in (25 × 5cm) mustard strips and stitch to the sides of the unit. Press the seams away from the middle.

4 With right sides together, place the 15 × 10in (38 × 25cm) mustard rectangle on top of the pillow front. Pin in place.

5 Stitch around each side, leaving a 3in (7.6cm) gap in the middle of the bottom seam. Trim the corners. Turn the pillow through the gap so that it is right side out. Press well. Using the cream embroidery thread and a running stitch (page 22), stitch the motifs to the pockets, ensuring that you only stitch through the top of the pockets and don't sew the pockets shut.

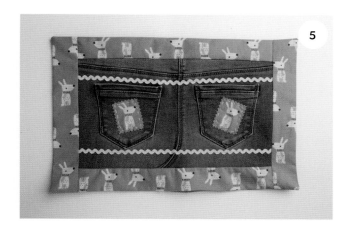

6 Stuff lightly with the polyester toy filling. Close the opening with small, neat slip stitches (page 22).

tips

• Customize the pillow with buttons or perhaps the embroidered name of the recipient or even a fairy or a tooth motif to the pockets.

• The design could be adapted to make a scented sleep pillow and be filled with lavender.

pencil case

A robust and hard-wearing pencil case for storing pens, pencils and other stationery items. This pencil case is a quick make with its metal zip, handy handle and shaped corners for extra storage room.

SIZE
4 × 8 x ½in (10 × 20.3 × 13mm) excluding handles

YOU WILL NEED
Denim
Two 5 × 9in (12.7 × 23cm) rectangles
One 2 × 5in (5 × 12.7cm) strip

Haberdashery
One 8in (20.3cm) zip
3in (7.6cm) navy ribbon ¼in (6mm) wide
Navy thread for piecing
Scissors, pins, ruler, marking pencil

PREPARATION
Small pieces of denim are needed for this project and they can be cut from any item of denim clothing.

1 Take the two 5 × 9in (12.7 × 23cm) denim rectangles and on one 9in (23cm) side of each rectangle, press under ½in (13mm) towards the wrong side of the fabric. Take the zip and pin it to one of the folded fabric edges so that the folded edge is ⅛in (3mm) away from the metal teeth of the zip. Repeat with the folded edge of the second rectangle.

2 Top stitch the zip in place using the navy thread.

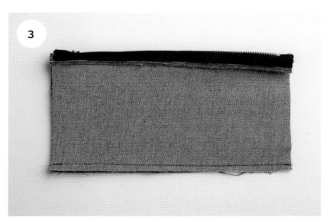

3 Fold the unit completed in step two in half with right sides facing and stitch down the long seam. Press the seam open.

4 To make the handle, take the 2 × 5in (5 × 12.7cm) denim strip and press under ¼in (6mm) on one long edge. On the opposite edge, press under ½in (13mm). Fold the ¼in (6mm) edge on top of the opposite folded edge so that it overlaps by ¼in (6mm). Pin in place, then top stitch close to the folded edge. Press. Stitch the raw ends of the handle strip to each side of the middle seam, on the zip-pull end, with an ⅛in (3mm) seam.

5 Open the zip halfway. With right sides together, keeping the zip in the middle on top of the middle back seam, stitch across each end. Stitch again ⅛in (3mm) away from the first line of stitching. To shape the corners, match the end seam with a side fold and on each side measure in ½in (13mm) from the end corner, draw a line across from edge to edge using the marking pencil. Stitch on the drawn line.

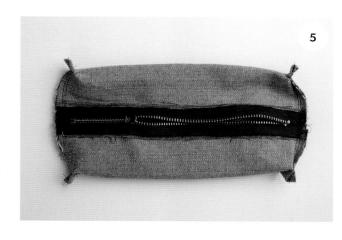

6 Turn the pencil case right side out. Push out the corners and press. Tie the 3in (7.6cm) piece of ribbon to the zip pull.

tips

• Substitute the ribbon on the zip pull for a trendy charm.

• To personalize the pencil case, embroider the name or initials of the recipient on one side.

tablet storage pouch

Keep your tablet or mini device safe when out and about with this softly padded pouch. The stylish trim contrasts with the dark denim while the quilting gives the pouch additional padding, ensuring that your device is well protected. The pouch is lined with wadding and a contrasting fabric and quilted with straight lines.

SIZE
8 × 10in (20.3 × 25cm)

YOU WILL NEED
Denim
One 8½ × 10½in (21.6 × 25cm) rectangle
Two 8½ × 4in (21.6 × 10cm) rectangles

Additional fabrics
Two 8½ × 10½in (21.6 × 26.7cm) rectangles navy print
One 8½ × 3½in (21.6 × 8.9cm) rectangle navy print

Haberdashery
Two 8½ × 10½in (21.6 × 26.7cm) rectangles fusible wadding
18in (45.7cm) navy ribbon ¼in (6mm) wide
One large button
Navy thread for piecing and quilting
Scissors, needle, pins, ruler

PREPARATION
Small pieces of denim are needed for this project so they can be cut from any item of denim clothing.

1 Place the two 8½ × 4in (21.6 × 10cm) denim rectangles with the 8½ × 3½in (21.6 × 8.9cm) navy print rectangle in between them. Stitch together the seams on the upper and lower edge of the print fabric to make one large rectangular piece. Press the seams open.

2 Iron the fusible wadding rectangles to the wrong side of the unit completed in step one and to the wrong side of the 8½ × 10½in (21.6 × 26.7cm) denim rectangle. Machine quilt each of these outer pouch units by stitching vertical lines across the pouch spaced 1in (2.5cm) apart.

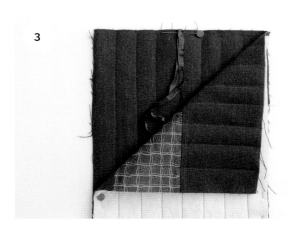

3 Fold the ribbon in half and pin it to the middle of the 8½in (21.6cm) raw edge on the right side of the plain outer pouch unit. Stitch the ribbon in place with an ⅛in (3mm) seam. With right sides together, pin the outer pouch sections together, leaving the top edge with the ribbon attached free.

4 Stitch around each side. Trim the corners and turn through. To stitch the lining take the two 8½ × 10½in (21.6 × 26.7cm) navy print rectangles and with right sides together stitch around three sides, leaving a 3in (7.5cm) gap in the stitching in the middle of one side. Trim the corners. Place the outer pouch inside the lining so that the right sides of the fabric are facing.

5 Matching the side seams and keeping the ribbon firmly tucked down, stitch around the top edge of the pouch. Turn through the opening and slip stitch (page 22) the gap in the lining closed. Carefully press the lining so that it sits ¼in (6mm) above the denim and pin in place. Stitch in the seam line.

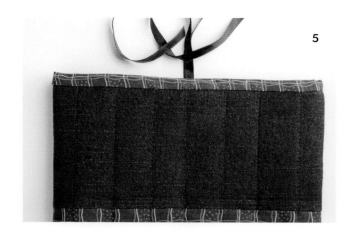

6 Stitch the button to the front of the pouch, positioning it 1½in (4cm) from the edge and in the middle. Tie the ribbon around the button.

tip

• The size of the tablet storage pouch can be adjusted to fit a device of any size. Simply measure the width and length of your tablet and add 2in (5cm).

wall hanging organizer

Keep everything neat and tidy with this wall hanging organizer. Perfect for letters, important papers, shopping lists, pens, pencils and other stationery items, with everything kept tidily in one place. The hanging unit is stitched from a large piece of denim with additional small and large pockets added.

SIZE
13½ × 26in (34.3 × 66cm)

YOU WILL NEED
Denim
One 14 × 26½in (35.6 × 67.3cm) rectangle including the top waistband
Two back pockets with at least 1in (2.5cm) denim around each side
One 4 × 5½in (10 × 14cm) front pocket
One 3 × 5in (7.6 × 12.7cm) part of a front pocket
One belt loop

Additional fabrics
One 14 × 26½in (35.8 × 67.3cm) rectangle grey print

Haberdashery
Navy thread for piecing
One 15in (38.1cm) wooden pole
25in (63.5cm) cord
Scissors, needle, pins, ruler

PREPARATION
The denim needed for this project came from a denim skirt. I chose to use a skirt as there was a lot of flat denim in the garment and the already attached pocket was a bonus, but any large piece of denim would be suitable. Additional front and back pockets cut from jeans and an extra belt loop will be needed.

1 Take the 14 × 26½in (35.8 × 67.3cm) denim rectangle and carefully unpick the top edge of the attached belt loop. Leave the bottom part of the loop attached to the denim.

2 Take the two back pockets and press under ¼in (6mm) on all edges. Pin the pockets to the 14 × 26½in (35.8 × 67.3cm) denim rectangle so that the pockets are placed ½in (13mm) in from the outer edge of the fabric and are facing towards the waistband on the denim. Check photo for placement.

3 Top stitch around the edges of each pocket with an ⅛in (3mm) seam. Take the two small front pockets and press under ¼in (6mm) on all edges. Pin in place, positioning these pockets in between the larger pockets. Top stitch around the edges of each small pocket with an ⅛in (3mm) seam.

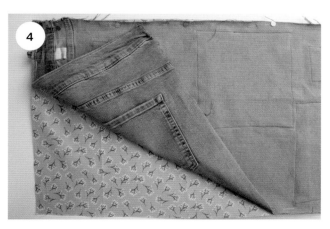

4 Stitch the bottom of the cut belt loop to the waistband so that it is opposite and in line with the existing loop. With right sides together, place the denim unit on top of the 14 × 26½in (35.6 × 67.3cm) grey rectangle. Pull the cut edges of the belt loops up so that they sit in the seam line and pin in place, then pin around the edges of the rectangle, leaving a 4in (10cm) gap in the bottom.

5 Stitch around each side, leaving the gap in the bottom. Trim the corners. Turn the unit through the gap so that it is right side out. Push out the corners and press well. Neatly slip stitch (page 22) the opening closed. Insert the pole through the belt loops and tie the cord to each end of the pole to create a hanger.

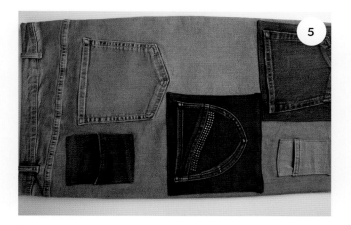

tip

• The hanging unit can be adapted to the denim available and the size of pockets. Alter the instructions to suit the sizes of the denim that you have to hand so that the unit can be made smaller or larger as desired.

three-in-a-row game

Great for when you are on the move, this game is a version of noughts and crosses and sure to become a family favourite. The square and oval buttons are used as counters and when not in use are stored in a pocket pouch. The playing mat is divided into nine squares with contrast trim and backed with a coordinating fabric.

SIZE
Playing mat 8½ × 8½in (21.6 × 21.6cm)
Storage pocket 6½ × 7¼in (16.5 × 18.4cm)

YOU WILL NEED
Denim
One 9in (23cm) square
One 7 × 7¾in (17.8 × 19.7cm) pocket including surrounding denim

Additional fabrics
One 9in (23cm) square beige print
One 7 × 7¾in (17.8 × 19.7cm) rectangle beige print

Haberdashery
44in (112cm) beige tape ½in (13mm) wide
Five large cream square buttons
Five large cream oval buttons
One small cream oval button
Black thread for piecing
Beige thread for top stitching
Scissors, needle, pins, ruler, marking pencil

PREPARATION
The denim needed for the playing mat can be cut from the leg of a pair of jeans. It is better if there are no seams as the mat needs to be flat and even. The pocket can be cut from the back of the jeans. Try and include at least 1in (2.5cm) of denim around the edges of the pocket for seam allowances.

1 To make the playing mat, cut the beige tape into four 9in (23cm) lengths. Take the 9in (23cm) denim square and, using the marking pencil, draw a grid across the square at 3in (7.6cm) intervals both horizontally and vertically. Place the tape over the marked lines, pin in place and stitch down each side of the tape.

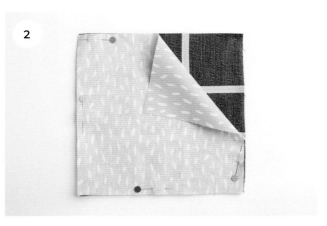

2 Take the 9in (23cm) beige print square and place it with right sides together on top of the unit completed in step one. Pin around the outer edge, then stitch around all four sides, leaving a 2in (5cm) gap in the stitching on one side. Trim the corners.

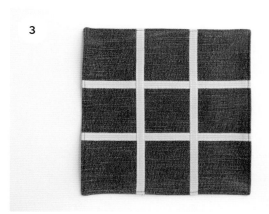

3 Turn the playing mat through the gap so that it is right side out. Push out the corners and press well. Top stitch ⅛in (3mm) away from the outer edge, closing the opening at the same time.

4 To make the pocket pouch, cut the remaining beige tape into a 5in (12.7cm) length. Fold in half and then pin the ends of the tape in line with the top edge of the pocket, positioning the tape in the middle of the pocket. Stitch in place using an ⅛in (3mm) seam.

5 Take the 7 × 7¾in (17.8 × 19.7cm) beige print rectangle and place it with right sides together on top of the unit completed in step four. Pin around the outer edge, then stitch around all four sides, leaving a 2in (5cm) gap in the stitching on one side. Trim the corners.

6 Turn the pocket pouch through the gap so that it is right side out. Push out the corners and press well. Top stitch ⅛in (3mm) away from the outer edge, closing the opening as you go. Stitch the small cream oval button to the top edge of the pocket, ensuring that you only stitch through the outer section of the pocket.

tips

• Felt squares and circles could be used for the counters instead of the buttons for an even lighter travel-friendly option.

• The game could be stored in the drawstring bag (page 66).

Templates

Note: Templates are
shown at 100%

Love cushion
(page 94)

Love cushion
(page 94)

Love cushion
(page 94)

Love cushion
(page 94)

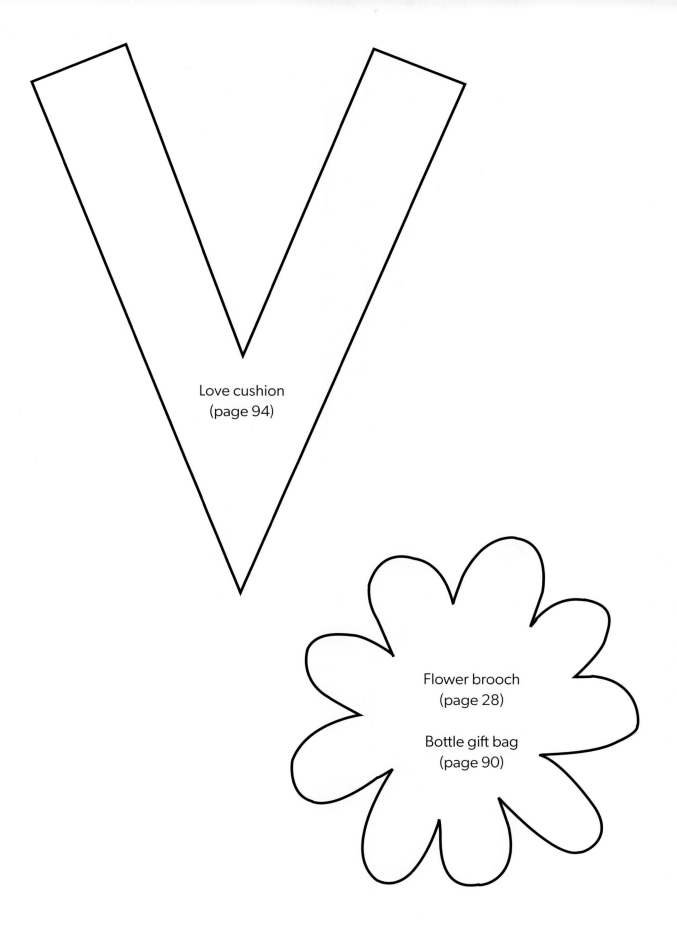

Love cushion
(page 94)

Flower brooch
(page 28)

Bottle gift bag
(page 90)

Home cushion
(page 98)

Home cushion
(page 98)

Home cushion
(page 98)

Home cushion
(page 98)

Hanging hearts
(page 106)

Index

GMC Publications Ltd
Castle Place, 166 High Street,
Lewes, East Sussex,
BN7 1XU
United Kingdom
Tel: +44 (0)1273 488005
www.gmcbooks.com